Wonderful Wild Animals

Fiona Kenshole

Name _____

Age _____

Class _____

OXFORD

UNIVERSITY PRESS

OXFORD
UNIVERSITY PRESS

Great Clarendon Street, Oxford OX2 6DP

Oxford University Press is a department of the University of Oxford.
It furthers the University's objective of excellence in research, scholarship,
and education by publishing worldwide in

Oxford New York

Auckland Cape Town Dar es Salaam Hong Kong Karachi
Kuala Lumpur Madrid Melbourne Mexico City Nairobi
New Delhi Shanghai Taipei Toronto

With offices in

Argentina Austria Brazil Chile Czech Republic France Greece
Guatemala Hungary Italy Japan South Korea Poland Portugal
Singapore Switzerland Thailand Turkey Ukraine Vietnam

OXFORD and OXFORD ENGLISH are registered trade marks of
Oxford University Press in the UK and in certain other countries

ISBN: 978 0 19 440104 3

Printed in China

ACKNOWLEDGEMENTS

The publisher would like to thank the following for their kind permission to reproduce the following:
Alamy Stock Photo pp 4 (dog/FogStock), 8 (squirrel/Zita Stankova), 10 (elephant/
Martin Harvey), 14 (bat/imageBROKER), 18 (lion/Greatstock), 22 (mouse/Colin Varndell);
Shutterstock pp 2 (polar bears/Anne Kiel), 6 (ducks/Randal Armstrong), 12 (camel/
marketa1982), 16 (crocodile/kavisimi), 20 (penguins/Roger Clark ARPS).
Cover image courtesy of Zita Stankova/Alamy Stock Photo
With thanks to Sally Spray for her contribution to this series

Reading Dolphins
Notes for teachers & parents

📖 Using the book

1 Begin by looking at the first story page (page 2). Look at the picture and ask questions about it. Then read the story text under the picture with your students. Use section 1 of the CD for this if possible.

2 Teach and check the understanding of any new vocabulary. Note that some of the words are in the **Picture Dictionary** at the back of the book.

3 Now look at the activities on the right-hand page. Show the example to the students and instruct them to complete the activities. This may be done individually, in pairs, or as a class.

4 Do the same for the remaining pages of the book.

5 Retell the whole story more quickly, reinforcing the new vocabulary. Section 2 of the CD can help with this.

6 If possible, listen to the expanded story (section 3 of the CD). The students should follow in their books.

7 When the book is finished, use the **Picture Dictionary** to check that students understand and remember new vocabulary. Section 4 of the CD can help with this.

💿 Using the CD

The CD contains four sections.

1 The story told slowly, with pauses. Use this during the first reading. It may also be used for "Listen and repeat" activities at any point.

2 The story told at normal speed. This should be used once the students have read the book for the first time.

3 The expanded story. The story is told in a longer version. This will help the students understand English when it is spoken faster, as they will now know the story and the vocabulary.

4 Vocabulary. Each word in the **Picture Dictionary** is spoken and then used in a simple sentence.

Wow! It's so cold today!

Yes. It's great weather for polar bears.

Why do polar bears like the cold?

They like to play in the snow.

What animals don't like the cold?

1 Complete the sentences.

❶ Polar bears ___are___ white.

❷ They _____ the cold.

❸ There are _____ polar bears in the photograph.

❹ The big bear _____ the mother.

❺ The mother is a very strong _____ .

❻ She _____ two cubs.

❼ _____ like to play in the snow.

❽ The snow is _____ and _____ .

2 Circle the words that describe a polar bear.

long   big   strong   thin
white   cute   hot   dangerous

Look! This dog doesn't like the cold.

It's a very cold, unhappy dog.

A dog's not a wild animal. Why doesn't it go inside by the fire?

It can't. It's a watchdog.

Make these sentences negative.

1 This is a bear.

This is not a bear.

2 The dog is very happy.

_____

3 It likes the cold.

_____

4 It can go inside.

_____

5 It is cold inside.

_____

6 It likes the snow.

_____

7 The snow is blue.

_____

8 This is a wild animal.

_____

Oh no! It's raining. We can't go outside to play.

I wish I was a duck.

A duck! Why?

Ducks like to play in the rain.

What animals don't like the rain?

1 Complete the sentences.

Jill: I wish I was a ___dolphin___ .

Tim: A ___dolphin___ !

    Why?

Jill: _Dolphins can swim_
in the sea. .

Tim: I wish _____

_____ .

Jill: A _____ ! Why?

Tim: _____

_____ .

2 Now write your own dialogue.

_____

_____

_____

_____

Look at this smart squirrel.

Smart? Why is it smart?

It's waiting under its umbrella.

What's it waiting for?

It's waiting for the rain to stop.

Connect.

It's waiting
for its food.

She's waiting
for the bus.

She's waiting for
the phone to ring.

He's waiting for
the green light.

He's waiting
to start.

He's waiting for
the rain to stop.

What's that elephant doing in the mud?

It's splashing mud on its body.

Why? It's getting very dirty.

No. It's keeping cool. Elephants love a mud bath.

Circle yes **or** no .

1. Elephants eat other animals.   yes (no)

2. Elephants can fly.   yes no

3. Elephants have big ears.   yes no

4. Elephants sleep standing up.   yes no

5. Elephants like snow.   yes no

6. Elephants weigh a lot.   yes no

7. Elephants put mud on their bodies to keep warm.   yes no

8. Elephants are the biggest land animal.   yes no

9. Asian elephants are bigger than African elephants.   yes no

10. The elephant's long nose is called a trunk.   yes no

Do camels like mud baths, too?

No. This camel likes sun and sand.

How does it live in the desert?

It does not need a lot of water, and it has big flat feet to walk on the sand.

Rearrange the words.

1 the   like   camels   sun

<u>Camels like the sun.</u>

2 in   camels   live   the   desert

_____

3 for   years   they   live   can   fifty

_____

4 has   a   flat   camel   feet   big

_____

5 a   three   camel   eyelids   has

_____

6 camels   big   tall   are   two   meters

_____

7 camel   the   one   African   has   hump

_____

What time is it?

It's night-time. The bats are flying around looking for food.

But it's so dark!

That's perfect for bats.

Circle the mistake and rewrite.

❶ Bats (comes) out at night.
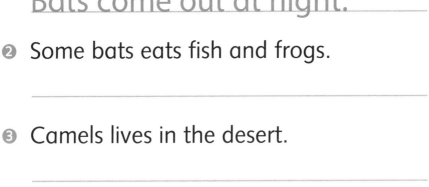
Bats come out at night.

❷ Some bats eats fish and frogs.

_____

❸ Camels lives in the desert.

_____

❹ An elephant splash mud on its body.

_____

❺ This dog want to go inside.

_____

❻ Ducks is happy in the rain.

_____

❼ This polar bear cub like the snow.

_____

❽ This squirrel don't like the rain.

_____

Sunshine is perfect for this crocodile.

Why does it like the sunshine?

It needs to warm up before it starts the day. It can't move quickly when it's cold.

Number.

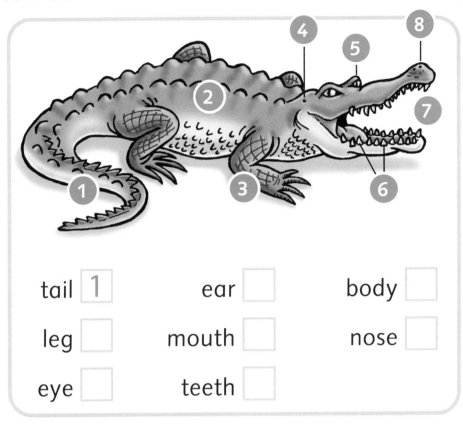

tail `1`   ear ☐   body ☐

leg ☐   mouth ☐   nose ☐

eye ☐   teeth ☐

Did you know?

- Crocodiles have cold blood.
- Crocodiles lay eggs.
- Crocodiles cannot see well under water.
- A mother crocodile carries her babies in her mouth.

Porcupines don't need to move quickly.

What do they do?

They use their spines. Nothing can hurt them.

What a great idea!

Answer the questions.

① Are porcupines very big?
<u>No, they are not.</u>

② Do porcupines have long spines?

_____

③ Can porcupines move quickly?

_____

④ Is this porcupine moving quickly?

_____

⑤ Does this porcupine have sharp spines?

_____

⑥ Is the lion afraid of the porcupine?

_____

⑦ Are porcupines dangerous?

_____

⑧ Do you like porcupines?

_____

Can you see the baby penguin?

It looks tired. Where does it sleep?

It can sleep anywhere on the snow.
Its parents bring it food.

Where do other animals sleep?

Circle the correct words.

1 Penguins can ~~cannot~~ fly.

2 Baby penguins is are cute.

3 Penguins has have wings.

4 Penguins lay egg eggs .

5 The baby penguin look looks tired.

6 Many penguins live in on Antarctica.

7 Baby penguins need their its parents.

8 Penguins like to is eat fish.

9 Penguins can swim very good well .

10 There is are seventeen types of penguin.

Polar bears sleep under the snow.
Squirrels sleep in a tree.
Crocodiles sleep by the river.
But this little mouse gets its rest
in a nice, warm, comfortable nest.

Complete.

I think _____animals_____ are

very _____cool_____ . The

_____ has its own umbrella.

_____ keep cool with mud.

_____ use the sun to warm

up. Baby _____ know where

it is safe to sleep. Nothing can touch a

_____ 's ball of spines.

_____ can live in a very hot

desert. _____ want it to rain

every day, and _____ can fly

at night. I like the _____

because _____

_____

_____ .

Picture Dictionary

bat

desert

bear

dolphin

camel

duck

crocodile

elephant

hump

snow

mouse

spine

nest

squirrel

penguin

trunk

porcupine

umbrella

Dolphin Readers

Dolphin Readers are available at five levels, from Starter to 4.

The Dolphins series covers four major themes:

Grammar, Living Together, The World Around Us, Science and Nature.

For each theme, there are two titles at every level.

Activity Books are available for all Dolphins.

All Dolphins are available on audio CD.
(2 TITLES ON EACH CD ☉ SEE TABLE BELOW)

Teacher's Notes are available at **www.oup.com/elt/dolphins**

	Grammar	Living Together	The World Around Us	Science and Nature
Starter	• Silly Squirrel • Monkeying Around ☉	• My Family • A Day with Baby ☉	• Doctor, Doctor • Moving House ☉	• A Game of Shapes • Baby Animals ☉
Level 1	• Meet Molly • Where Is It? ☉	• Little Helpers • Jack the Hero ☉	• On Safari • Lost Kitten ☉	• Number Magic • How's the Weather? ☉
Level 2	• Double Trouble • Super Sam ☉	• Candy for Breakfast • Lost! ☉	• A Visit to the City • Matt's Mistake ☉	• Numbers, Numbers Everywhere • Circles and Squares ☉
Level 3	• Students in Space • What Did You Do Yesterday? ☉	• New Girl in School • Uncle Jerry's Great Idea ☉	• Just Like Mine • Wonderful Wild Animals ☉	• Things That Fly • Let's Go to the Rainforest ☉
Level 4	• The Tough Task • Yesterday, Today, and Tomorrow ☉	• We Won the Cup • Up and Down ☉	• Where People Live • City Girl, Country Boy ☉	• In the Ocean • Go, Gorillas, Go ☉